An I relays the story in its not-story way. With traces of story. The sound is uniquely of its city in a nearly, not-named way. Attuned to its humidified breezes and the fan blade's indispensable turning. Home is the sole locale, the nucleus, ever so. The voice struggles 'to end its own noise,' not to inventory only regrets and losses, rattled and battered; cycling through the dead, friends and kin, pictures, 'the stalactites of memory' and bars in which years must have passed, stumbled through, a survivor, "godly,/of one mind, learning too late whatever/was on offer, outlasting fabulous destinies…" A work, a worksong, not of an illusory life, but of a life, in a body, a family, on wheels, rubber-side down, that works, miraculously.

—C.D. Wright,
author of *One With Others*,
National Book Critics Circle Award winner

Ralph Adamo has lived his three-score-plus years in New Orleans. To say that the poems in Ever are about that city of the dead, the dying, and the coming-to-be would be a great disservice. These are the poems of man who has become his city. To be sure, the jazz, the floods, the drunks, and the turbulence of despair are here, but they exist in the words of one who has absorbed them into himself. If "the blinked-smile the non-survivor wears / toward peace" describes one overwhelmed by it all, Adamo, ever looking forward, brings comfort, like words whispered in the ear of a drowsy child.

—R.S. (Sam) Gwynn,
author of *No Word of Farewell: Poems 1970-2000*

Reading Ralph Adamo's poetry puts you in a courtly brooding world where the truth comes driving through the gloom like elegance. You picture him "standing absolutely motionless at a slight angle to the universe," as E.M. Forster described Cavafy.

—Nancy Lemann,
author of *Lives of the Saints*

For more than forty years, while "arguing words against / The constant threat: forgetting," Ralph Adamo has published poems as original as any I know. In his seventh collection, Ever, in which sometimes "a word is as far from a fact / as fever can burn it," a speaker whittles "the little lies down to / The nuance of perfect teeth in a closed mouth." Another speaker whispers to his young children, "My children are exhausting" and "'riddle' means 'dark language'" in order to help spirit them to bed. In another poem, retrospection makes a speaker "sag like an old bookshelf and sigh like the door beyond it." And in another, a speaker prays for adolescent boys in their lostness—"world without hearing, amen." Such phrasings hint at greater recognitions to come—for instance, that poetry is "just listening to the world." What may be most original and satisfying about the thirteen years of poems in Ever is that reading and rereading them is to experience the art and diverse craft of a master, one who would wince at the accolade and never accept it.

—Randy Bates,
author of *Rings: On the Life and Family of a Southern Fighter*

In Ever, Ralph Adamo has focused his poetic lens on the small moments that make life bittersweet and profound. Whether he is describing the banter of children at play or words uttered on a deathbed, Adamo puts the reader in the room and hands him a magnifying glass. The poet is asking us to watch life closely as it swiftly passes. He gives very specific metaphors of pain, familiar to any New Orleanian "like stinging caterpillars down from ghostly cocoons en masse to prey on the bare feet of us all." The book contains many precisely chosen words and well-considered passages. But he also offers some less concrete, more esoteric and slightly sardonic observations "Some things have always fallen through time and space to land god knows where."

Adamo writes confidently about the value in dysfunction and skeptically about pure redemption. "I was going to get older someday. I was going to blame somebody." Sometimes the work seems so personal that it should be reworked in the reader's mind. In "Visiting the Marker, After the Flood," the narrator asks "What did you expect to happen clawing through the chicken wire at the top of the 20th century." To understand this poem about death and life, the reader must step back and watch the words flow past.

Adamo's narrator laments the people who have disappeared without ceremony. He names them in a list broken by undisguised feelings – among them that he cannot properly remember all the names. But the spirits of the dead emerge and disappear throughout the book, allowing readers the experience of tangible and fleeting memories too.

Written in dense beautiful language, Ever is about temporal, conscious and self-conscious experiences. Underlying Ever is a question of whether we will find the perfect afterlife. This is a book without any neat, simple answers. Still, Adamo seems to be telling us that happily ever after, our Ever, is here.

—Fatima Shaik,
author of *The Mayor of New Orleans: Just Talking Jazz*
and *What Went Missing and What Got Found*

ALL THE GOOD HIDING PLACES

POEMS

WORKS BY RALPH ADAMO

POETRY

The Tiger Who Spoke French
Why We Have Friends
Sadness at the Private University
The End of the World
Hanoi Rose
Waterblind
Ever: Poems 2000-2014

EDITOR

Big Easy: An Anthology of New Orleans Poetry (1978)
American Waste by Everette Maddox
Whatever Passes for Love is Love by John Stoss
I Hope Its Not Over And Goodby: Selected Poems of Everette Maddox

ALL THE GOOD HIDING PLACES

POEMS

RALPH ADAMO

BLACK
WIDOW
PRESS
BOSTON

Black Widow Press is an imprint of Commonwealth Books, Inc., Boston, MA. Distributed to the trade by NBN (National Book Network) throughout North America, Canada, and the U.K. Black Widow Press and its logo are registered trademarks of Commonwealth Books, Inc.

Joseph S. Phillips and Susan J. Wood, Ph.D., Publishers
www.blackwidowpress.com

Cover design & text production: Geoff Munsterman
Cover image: "Contrejour" by Josephine Sacabo

ISBN-13: 978-1-7338924-2-1

Printed in the United States of America

10 9 8 7 6 5 4 3 2 1

TABLE OF CONTENTS

II. UNCLAIMED BODIES

ALL THE GOOD HIDING PLACES

I. THE ASKING

I don't care how many letters they sent—
the morning came the morning went

Play what you feel, if that's how you feel it—
don't ask for too much unless you're willing to steal it

—*"When You Stay Strong"*
Lisa Mednick Powell

The Last Thing We Ever Do

No one is there, no one is coming
from miles around, the elements favor
the shade across the way, as always.

Fine edge of restraint, hand in hand,
looking for the place not there and
before you know it not anywhere.

Maybe I even knew it, evidence in
writing suggests I might have
known in the helpless way of one

dropping through false flooring
about any heart's many discrepancies,
perplexing grief ahead and behind,

and how aligned perfection is
with loss. We want to shout I
love you until thin air releases

us. I say this cautiously, left among
confusion so pure a rare numeral
breaks over me receding...

Of which recollections none
have skeletal form but mere enfolding
fuels that prey and prey and prey.

DYING DANCING

I ask the noise I've asked to join me to disjoin abruptly causing
the remains of confusion to advance three steps lightly, for love
was where when I went I wanted to go or thought I'd gone
the slimmest whistling catches the woebegone throat
whereupon silence takes root, long, deep, mesmerized
struggle in which crepe myrtle and oak figure, and willow and
the vine of the mirliton, how many nights is this many
years, gone murmuring dawn and kindled light—

across the puny dividend space makes, below a taut
measure of ecru flesh, so layered craft winnows, bucks,
affords unalloyed movement within, watches, waits
for waiting to begin. It is more than an hour, less
than a lost lifetime I rise to reach this under
standing of or is it with, an hour broken unshared
dreams recall while all interior lifting winds rain
down the end of the end of you always beginning

A PARTIALLY COHERENT MESSAGE TO MY CHILDREN

Christmas will belong to you one day,
and if I'm anywhere, if I'm lucky, I might
be a thought in a mirror, nothing more

There is no doubt this is the world we live in,
we who have taken ourselves to the side of great events
and fortunes, who have substituted human drama for the public stage,
subject and author of stories,
crucial cartilage, self-loading systems, one with and from
our beginnings, the sum of memories—none of them remembered—

deep in the cocoon of the national security state sorting out problems so small
their seismology rejects inspection
while war gurgles from children's mouths and the apparatus rewires

Here we turn the small things over in our hands our heads between our teeth in our
stomachs? well, or not well, but moving on
always, the quid of the pro the quo the quotidian where
we do live, off in the cool shadow, our pockets pure functionality...

(A girl crouched near water
  shooting pictures of ducks)

But what does the chest know?
or the cognac for that matter, or the writing desk
bearing an apiaries history within its dusty odor?

I used to go alone and come back alone.
I'd bring my own supplies, was
not looking for surprise.
Just music.

So much time written into those songs—

You say a thing IS a thing, not
LIKE a thing, which makes the whole thing smaller,
and when you have to sleep on it
you'd better have your dog by your side.

Brown Cow

What—I can finally think—will be the last
memory to go? Though when I say it like this
I imagine an image being delivered
for a modest tip. But serious too will seem
the final dispatch from a place so overrun
with other intentions, I hesitate summoning
so set up a set-up showdown epic set
piece of wonder lust and blank space
(unforced error: me) oh let all dance
loose on this heavy heavenly heaving, I'll
swan, there was a point sharp enough pokingly
to swim a span of swelter seething soberly.
Oh, the modifications, their endearing nethers
twined, worm-skewed, puppy loved, the ripple
of welcome water a cool promise, otherwise
and wasn't she? After all who will come but
that whom the dream possessed who held a few
facecards, who bluffed like an angel, cooed
like a baby snake, wondrously unaccountable—
taking it all back retreating with rare courage
I am no doubt not going to see a thing. Then.
Now. How the divide multiples. How now.

The Bulge

My father should have had better, is what I think,
is what I've always thought; it's my complaint,
not his. I never heard him grouse about fate, his
lot, the kinds of things men whine about,
reeling in their catch in greedy spurts.
My father was calm, even when provoked,
Measured, *a battuta* at least, & *andante*.

Mud is bad enough if you're naturally neat.
And cold that slices thin cuts in your soul.
Put the two together and add gunfire, razor
wire, mortars blowing trees to kingdom come,
no toothbrush, socks wet for days on end
inside of shoes there is no one to mend—
the inside of the brain wavers and wends—
but isolation crowds discomfort, misery
corners the rocky landscape, starburned.

⚜⚜⚜

I try to picture my old man as an old man
My friends all passing my father's final age
Like travelers past an unseen stone

My father who dug holes in French dirt, or was it German?
No one knew anything except the wind tore the flesh from their faces, except the
chill was like weeds blooming in the blood from feet all the way up to ears, except
who could feel their ears? The ice spoke each man's name slowly, crystalized in one
eyeball after another, except face-down in the dirt was blind luck, except a man was
repeating his mother's name and it was the same as the name of the man's mother
next to him, in the dirt that had no country carved into it, or had had none or
would have...

My father turns from the barbed wire where hangs the flesh of who knows whom or
from which side, hangs like rags this flesh still damp still marked by small cuts and
dirt dripping from the wire like paper mâché drying, a still life sliced from irony.

LOCAL MURDERS

I

I was in a competition to see who could respond to and withstand psychological and supernatural torture/torment the best. There were 5 or 6 tests—one had me mentally concentrating on what would be for me the 'perfect life.'

I was aware the pitfalls of this one would be too much emphasis on material success. I focused really hard on a bucolic sort of happiness, surrounded by loved ones and 'meaning.' As the test ended I became aware of a slow moving train pushing into me and moving me along ahead of it, up a sort of long long picnic table, never really hurting me, and then gently depositing me at a table where all the people sitting around we're my own dead (though I mainly remember my father and sister) none looking too good, but their appearing dead didn't frighten or bother me, and I spoke to them and touched them.

I remember thinking I must have done well with the tests.

II

Her vapor trail like the four-o'clocks of memory, sweetening every fence between school and home.

III

Among the self-incited exits, John Pardue arrives cold one morning by phone: as he'd lived his last few years alone trailing the distant noise of wives and daughters and back of that his own mother, dead too early, and his hard but sympathetic dad...

he had little room left for himself,

Transient, Viking, king of the law. Hard monkey. Muscles layered over brains—why shoot this man, John, my friend, who taught me rudimentary tough,

and did not stint a bit on it?

THE UNEXPECTED STATES OF AMERICA

These are not the joys we are looking for

Whoever does not think he is at the center of the universe is mistaken,
or she is who could not hear
the one wind-conducted voice

Hearing my son walk in the hall tonight, I pause reading and look up,
feel my face form to my father's features, a countenance awaiting my acceptance.

a blue like hope
lattice shadow
drowned word

music of tables
in sunshine

If I ever did...
But I never would...

If I ever did...
But I never would...

I don't think Steve Mistretta meant to be a bully. That he looked to us like Frankenstein's
    monster—stiff, big and nearly dumb—might account for why we acted scared at
    his approach,
and...oh,
Karen Doyle's crisp white blouse would tent between the second and third button
    where her small brown nipple stood

Known for grim soul-clutching vanity
& the secret will of milk

You go to the coffee shop
to see flesh and drink blood

Learning to live in the world where you find yourselves
Everything moves forward
past the shallow ground where the hero lies

Where he marks
the unfamiliar history of yesterday
recalled if at all in passing

So many years to have kept it all unspoken—even largely unremembered—
    counting on it
being where I could find it
one day when, as they say,
the day came...

Jack Gilbert Underground

Strange to be home
touching all the edges of the dark
with more fingers than I remember—
I speak I find the language of the root
scavenging sound through organ
after organ—how many times
the air welcomed me like an old
friend troubling the hidden tongue
and now the countercurrent—

stiches of shadow and the cracked
full moon tugging white hairs red—
the mouth I no longer open
hungers for a word to say, salivates
(I make a joke on salvation) but
it's true the moisture rises under
the missing tongue at the idea of
'you,' such a clear and clever word
it elevates the dark already dig-
nified, anarchic, grievously
gloriously itself apart from light...

what did I do before I did this lying
in the dark? my hands beheld
their work but what had I made
that weighs so heavy pressing
the quiet like a form of me
down hard, harder, hardest
where the heart once released
its numberless song?

RING DANCE

My life is full of titles these days, but

Once my poems were so drunk
they could barely stand, and though
it might sound like bragging to say
their headaches were legendary, it is
not bragging, believe me. I was there.

But the dialogues that ensued!
I recall when my poems spilled beer
(they were poor) on Rette's elegant sleeve...

Because you are either right or wrong, the details can go to hell.

Is a poem worth so many nights uncovered? The asking asks.

I got right down into the heart as if trying to survive without hope.
It was a tight fit.

Pre-Sleep

It is threatening to rain, we say,
a classic case of when an antecedent
would come in handy, and why
such a threat should be leveled
at innocents like us—well, it
is the innocent who suffer, isn't
it? more than the ones with
ridges and grooves

Ambition, desire, need—
let's pull them apart, like muscles
that have pathologically entwined and head

for the dreamscape of the day before

or maybe just bed, where after a while
the things we see with our eyes closed—the open eyes,
the clenched face, the crowd growing aerially smaller, a
point so lit the closed eye burns with it, then fear, then
grief, until at last the human beast gives out and sleep
arrives like an old body putting one foot forward to stumble
against all the years piled atop the river running blue

—uncompromising old age, storm unto death—

how ordinary we survivors seem
claiming the earth's surface, accepting the sun as given...

If Jesus

If Jesus had lived to be 60 would he feel at all as I do sometimes?
Tired a little too early in the day. Feet hurting. Cherished
Beliefs dimming on the tide of practical developments,
Not enough scratch to keep everyone happy, bad
Dreams in a bed grown lonely...I mean,
At thirty three I had some vision left if no plan,
Believed in love's inevitable triumph, despite
Every setback to the contrary to that time, most
Surely including all my own failures to see
People for whom they were...

Seconds

There is meaning and then there is
the need for meaning,
the paint maker's art curiously syntactic.
The romance of numbers
slipping into place. If fate is always hybrid
who can become both sane and
moral? When earth was born, vagabond & pitifully turned out, already it had fathers
laying down marching orders and a sun
unjust, disquieted to the core.
Who has the strength anymore to be
terrifying? A reflection twice removed calms falsely while all hell rebels.

Odors of grass and dirt in the Spring heat.
Memory no longer required unless you want to make sense out of what you know.

The very idea. Form of the formula. Twice and then once and then—

But you and I had stopped talking.
Whoever and I too had ceased to say.
To form the bridge that
...ok, you step up one then another then and on and on, the noises that would stop
    you do not and up you go, onward for the nonce, but none of that equals
the energy of the cat in the place the cat
would flee. Thinking over it—

weeds with the sap of thin blood and berries that crush to a darker shade.

The embodied and the tag along.

The mishmash of memory
rarely leads to the poem of joy.

Senses petrified, I regain my prolonged assumptions. No drool of language hangs
    from my lips—geometric supplication.
Anger. Sleep.
                Remember why a slave would lie, even in his song, even in
her song. Form following habitat.

Sooner or later I'll have to confess
that I can't do everything I do,
that the gap between intention and completion widens like a predator's mouth
    at dusk, that all promises have been or are being broken.

                 Even if I could have dreamed more furiously, my dreams—
heroic, conclusive, honest—disappear at the morning sink. And are no use
on this troubled plane. And weigh down my need to rise above complaint,
disappointment, envy.

    It is possible to be glad all matter is the same age, whomever it is stuck to for
however long and whenever it was dealt...

    ❖❖❖

Endless boasting in the face of death
has made us tired, and more afraid.

Diary of Wind and Weather

Looking now
I wonder what I see—
The open mouth of the rain, yes, but
its small breaths too. I always
want to be siding with people who believe
and are not crazed by their belief.
That is almost to say
young people, and musical people, and those who have had
their hearts broken
over and over and noticed.

The things we are not, the things
we didn't do, the world of us who say this
in our sleep.
            The painter to the garden yields, and the singer dwells in the desert.
While I have neither half of a mind
to share.

❖❖❖

The wren perched on the weather clock describes in his song the shape of the
    wind, whose magnetism draws us toward the rings of Saturn. Or so the clock's
    longitudes led us to believe, sitting sexually upon a chair in a house, like all
    houses, that was not ours.

Surface anatomy! Near Naples, in a stew of languages, my ancient father toiled at
    his habitual syncretizing. There in the dark narrow shell of the parallelogram, he
    found the mouth of the underground ocean, my birthright, my gift to you.

❖❖❖

Forced by biology to live among the young,
you may lose the thread of the spirit that has gotten you
this far—not the horrors of unheard music or mere strangeness
like tattooed arms&legs—but that old conversation about spirituality from new,
    painfully sweet-looking lips.
That hurts harder than incineration.

SEEING SUNNY AFTER FOURTEEN YEARS

We brush our stubbly cheeks. He knows
what he's doing now: kissing his baby
brother. Here's one more goodbye, but
who's leaving whom? and where is anyone
going? The afternoon feels like a long sit
down, a wait, a listen but the noise has no
inflection, like a breeze it slips past slips
past slips—on the air scents of supper.

Dialogue for Novel: Title: The One Who's Looking

"It's not a world I don't want to live in;
it's a world I don't know how to live in."

I was allowed only imaginative access to house,
boards, bedrooms, the moist, sweet
& sour undergarments of the dancer

From when do I count the end of my life in love?
Me love life is it over?
Is it true I'm no longer a lover?

If history teaches us anything, it's not to trust ourselves.

She'll isolate you and gut you, but no one
ever ends the way they do in movies or
even books unless they're dead, in which
case, ended. The rest go on, oh maybe
limping, maybe even mortally wounded
at least somewhere in their heads (the
internal version of 'Dead Man'), but on
they go, changing, running into new
reasons to hope or despair, to have
another drink, another try at sexual
satisfaction (you may find it grim but no
one gives this up without a fight)...
The dreaded conclusion does not necessarily
close the deal is all I'm trying to say.
The world is full of characters given up long
ago by someone, or by everyone, but
usually by someone we (they'd) call
'special.'

Like you, for instance, monster of my heart,
keeper of my dream life, pastor who
gave up on God without telling the rest of us,
red-lipped one, innocent to a very
deep fault, my end that failed to kill me off clean.

No longer obsessed with a woman from each past.

Layers and layers of undreamed sleep
slide between those years and this and yet
—when I pull out the chair to sit it is as if
less than three days have passed (how our
dreams mock us, whether or not we need
mocking), and I am mouthfuls of forgotten
speech, a whole dictionary of desire I do
not yet know is useless...

This Is Now

Mine is sensual and forlorn,
Jones all humanist and half divine,
Leon so angry through spitting laughter,
Sam sad, born to look away, eyeballs
like gritted teeth, and Stoss—luxuriant
lover exhaled by long-departed deities...
the women I did not understand (as they
have known since first light), nor
the singing man still standing knife deep in
his heart that cannot bleed. We spoke
on mountaintops, it's true, low mountains,
but more in late-night diners, and cars
unfit for the road, declaring too on porches,
the smoky room, yards only nature kept.
One of us missed those early end times,
these memories, honorary, aloof, untrue,
but should've been there, not half so
lost as we few in that day, scared to the
breaking point, closing in on it.
We could have used the cloth, some
honeyed breathing, and the rest.

COFFEESHOP READING JONES

The three girls I cannot help but
look at cannot help but
look away, and thus
the male gaze marks me,
although I would not have it so—would
what? become more subtle? invisible?
What will end well has not yet
been thought up. Instead, I see
her, about whom the thing of true
(and truly fabulous) interest is the way
her haunting rump joins her tender thighs,
which my useless consciousness
continually objectifies. If I could breathe
on you as God did mud, I would, and
would in a single breath communicate
(or try, try) a sense closer
to understanding and love, were love
on the table, or at the very least,
appreciation without the stain of meaning
it so hard I cannot suck back this wind
steering my errant soul.

Past Imperfect

Center around the ambient sound,
under and no more—handled blind—
refusing to be smoothed. You have been
a figure of speech, after love, and I
was there, leaf on a mountain road, never
to listen, much less hear, a longing
worse than ever meeting again.

If god was murdered the news was slow
to reach our camp. We went about
the business of the slaughter like pros,
fires unplumbed—old as your departure,
the timely dreamt impression quiet
as song slipping its pattern. Within
the chant, the morning after all, all.

I could not tell myself a thing truer
than your trouble, our dance. Desire
without scar. *Obligato*! Content with killing
and running late, hardened post-decay,
morning knees, hair spread for combing,
heart stained like a child's bedroom wall
with too much unencumbered thought.

Ah-ha

Son of Joe Adamo watching
Metropolis in Natchitoches
on a Saturday morning in July.

(Not sitting on the grass in Jackson Square
eating black olives from a jar, pronounced:
'decadent' by C.D., who then had another.)

Our parents sometimes leave us
in the strangest places, as do
our friends, as may our kids.

As many times as I've said
'look at this,' I think maybe
I never saw it myself,

What's in a laugh?
Does an ancient wind
unloosed from its galaxy

depart the guilty mouth, once
affixed on nourishment
at all costs, and away?

Unclaimed Bodies

Our house has gone under, our horses our pigs
the first day everything has to be perfect
through this red algae, a beautiful part, pulling water
into its system.   Is anyone still here?
You discover it deep below the surface
    (the ship's lights almost lost in the fog, music rising
sternly down she gazed until my hand fell away from the other's throat)
to think that I painted you. But I am like that still.
I'm hoping to share this light to be full
to the roots the whole city came she left
her water and went into the city.
Now baby...the wind and rain is starting to subside...
    (emotive in the extreme my countryman singing
the one that you requested most someday of the days
that come you will come and remind me...)
took it real hard kind of lost my mind a little
music is like medicine a lot of responsibility
on a scale that's never before been
one of the triangle's great mysteries
you feel quantum vivid conductors
but I also have a thing they don't have if you have died—
was it his idea a bird in a drawer what you're talking about
for the rest of his life the end in the book
before she died in the end he comes back
where you walk in there's blue there's yellow, red you
don't have to worry about waking yourself up here's what happened.
All of the sudden it was the wrong size
a necklace you never take off we never get to see
we just want to make sure you all know
on your very first day look how beautiful these things are
to resolve a generous portion every step of the way—
many variations of blue I didn't have to do anything
we have seen the predictions
but something woke me up on a collision course
like a nuclear explosion looking for somebody and if so
what can I do about it nothing convenient just a hit in the dark
a lot of dancing what was it like now that you've gone through it what
do you want to be remembered for—

so he's pushing down on that surface
if you haven't thought of it before
So we know ancient civilizations and astronomers
on this side of the house are you kissing the tree
What the hell happened there? not talked to in years the day to day
some place somehow no place to go if you fail to do something about it

Start with Black, Move to Blue

Here is the garden where the bitter end begins
Not a war from the middle out
And not too much of a good thing
Not a bad smell from everywhere
Life lived as through a phantom limb
Head to toe
Brain to balls

When I think of all the things I was afraid to do in my life
I get seasick, turned around and then inside out with it
The moonlit swim not taken
The music never uttered from my lips, fingers
So many easy ways out taken
When there was pain to be wrestled

Still to be accused of not having suffered—that was painful, shocking, not
even true, but all it took it seemed to mark
conclusion & despair. Because the fear
was real as was the cowardice.
And now beholden
every which a way, complicit, re-
resigned, too many la's to the
dah, what's there to say?
That's what I thought, I said.

The Poem Is a Myth Take

...and just like that the bad habit went
away.

...to make something beautiful out of
confusion and despair.

...to say out loud these things that don't
add up.

...whatever fits you trying to come off.

Where is that window love flew through,
and what branch could hold its sorry carcass?

...to imagine in the grip of water the depth
of the sun.

...an ersatz cousin named Inky, no mark on
him, nary a tat or a too...

...my grandmother's voice scratchy, but
from what? she didn't smoke, I never
heard her shout...

...starting from the word zero, and the
number not.

...to do a brave thing whether the
moonlight's off or on...

How little kindness is left at the end of the
chord.

Cicatrization

Eccentrics, castoffs, drifters...
being liable to create expectations
all opposites in the maternal body, the
dream-soul...fearing to become too strong
the brother who looks toward the jungle—
toward the overarching logic of death...
Operating on the prophetic plane I entered
the common area. I wish to say that it hurt.
We built shelters of cedar heating the
sun's echo...the elder world vanished.
Mathematical precision must not interfere.
The gift of water, the light of the theurgist.
At the end of our days only the strategies
survive...but you do not forgive me.

CONVERT

Discipline = punishing yourself

While it's true I was rarely the smartest
person in the room, it is also true
I knew how to suffer in silence.

Years might pass
without the sound
that revealed me.

But alive in some memories—that
memory—one cannot see out, feeling
being all, trapped there growing a future
horribly beautiful and despair without wings ...

Subtract the absence
bury the remainder
time the hold and
will the consequences.

Who doubts the turned over card bloodied
at the intersection

Making Like

The prow of a ship dissolving like blood in water

Shoulder bared, not as teeth are or trees become

I never once thought of leaving home

Such times arrive
as cause

He has a smile but when he goes
to laugh he can't

I set things down
I set them down
My book my phone my old way home

Me and the moon and the man I am

FELO DE SE

The grid of hours the skin of minutes the
microscopic world of seconds

The year of terrible pain and crazy
optimism

I am lying in a bed of stars
There is no reason

There you are
Brighter than all comfort most despair

I see I cannot see
You anywhere but here

Morning That Held Sway

Naked and fearless as only a child can be
Not yet snared by a sense of decency
I want to hold my hand up to the sky
To see the passing of others as a way
Of being less lonely than before—
The air was darker than memory
What I can recall, foxes in the morning
Barking at the sun, that much
Optimism, for a throwback a life
Time. So there I was, me away
From home, longing for a home
(Yes, a son of Capitalism) when
The worth of nothing struck me—
I don't want to say 'dumb' but close—
I sought in vain for comedy, land
Scapes haunted my imagination,
First the sun then the moon looked
To rise from my palm, the horses
That rode off were riding back, so
Many had disappeared, in the meantime.

SOMETHING WITH NUMBERS

Twenty years away from that first glance
wresting me awake
to clear away regret
a flattened dream for the given dance
no diagrams   the universe

returns my head to its upright position

A hard cold sadness settles
Not one I don't know
None I can't absorb
Dreams that won't
See it my way

There was no cause to love you simply
Too bright like the star we worship

Talking was endless and useless
Body to body—nothing to be taken or given back—
All as well ends

Words like knives
Thrown at the moon

Making Time i

I enter the light ten times
On the ninth you say wait

The world is this way look
A vessel raining vows

Inexhaustible heart
Gardens ponds and streams

Space clear and false
Under canopies eons eyes

And yet even so still
You say wait just there

Where you are we are
Afflictions moon and stars

Making Time II

The life we seem to have
In the house at odds with itself

Does not dance cannot do math
Reads at a lower level and cries

Itself awake from dreams animals
Are buried in.

                        This is as serious
And so useless: the girl in the bakery

Some forty odd years back whose
Finger brushed electric with the change,

May I see her? Sixty now and still
(I can see this but how?) the ingénue,

Slender, with fine hair and innocent
As the goods she sold. I wrote

The flakes of a poor poem then,
As now, to honor this fleeting longing

About which it must be better
Not to speak, as I did not then,

Driving home suddenly alone,
Though still young, my life ahead of me.

FEELING SORRY FOR THE DICTATOR'S SONS

I'm sorry
but when I heard the reports
of the way the dictator's sons were hunted down and murdered
by crowds nursing thirty years of anger over thirty years of abuse (well,
or the American military)

I felt bad for them
Guilty no doubt of their own horrors
Of their murdering moments and
Terrible crimes particularly
Against women, but

Crimes born of the opportunities
Their births arranged and pretty much
Guaranteed...I felt sorry
(Though my own brother said No
that's a mistake)

Two guys who owned the world from day one
Raised to the *nth* of the id
Schooled in torture, rewarded with
little palaces of their own and the girls of every village—vile as humans come,
    but...

Uday and Qusay—frat boys raised to the magnitude of suns...

When the old man was finally dragged from his hole, was that a tear dribbling
    down his beggar's beard and was it for himself alone?

A man is walking a dog and juggling words in his head. Has he forgotten
that human beings are the measure of pain?

POEM NEAR A FAR BIRTHDAY

I feel lonely sometimes when I'm on my own,
and want my mom and dad to come get me,
especially my dad,
whom I called 'daddy,' not dad.
What am I
doing anywhere is what I wonder.

An unhinged look past the edges of trees—
cushion of all time pushing softly
against my eyes—the moment they see
something they cease the journey—eyes
carol confirm conform conclude all in
a timely time not yet beat bloody by memory—
hosannas, sweltering beneath the tongue—
these trees and I require so little,
but they less, my hungers filling the simple air—
crossings—the sun recalling itself to the fire—
birds aborning—

Looking backwards is the rainy season,
mute warbling, a weight of air drying
in the space between your eyes—
Never to come back, having never
been gone.

PREWRITING ISAAC'S ELEGY
for Kay

Although it's a crap shoot which one of us
goes first, it is a fact that both of us will go.

If me, your only elegy might be sometimes
a mystified low growl—dog for question,

If you, well, I know I'll be too bummed
to make a good bowl of words drop

from my suddenly quiet mouth—
you might get one, an elegy, eventually,

composed of meaty memory, old bones,
the scent of cat to cause your tongue

to drool; sure, I'd put all that in for you.
But first—see I'm a wreck, sleepless,

lonely, ready for a stroll we can't take...
Even now, you're barely middle-aged and

I feel a swell in the back of my throat.
No one lives forever though some try,

the rope-a-dope with death always ending
in the knockout. But dogs are different,

like Rilke says, the shadow spares them.
You walk enmeshed in scent, your worries

not nothing but not abstract. Sleep heals
what ails, and food, and staying near.

This closeness not mere intermission
after all, good dog, doodle, Isaac, friend.

The Big Now

I've walked past too much beauty, so
much my natural name must be 'He who
walks past beauty, barely looking up'

It seems an odd time to feel abashed
at every turn—

Don't get me wrong—
I knew what money was,
I just couldn't reach any

Connoisseur of voices
I leave myself cold, left
I should say, left and right

While the obverse may be worse, how many
people can't take their own selves
seriously? Paralyzed by their
reflections in which all flaws shine...

I heard the music making the rounds.
It had on an old coat, holey,
and feet stuck in thin slippers.

So many solutions
In which to dissolve
the notes that held nothing back—
a flute of sunlight
cradles incipience...
small cracks filter forward
until I have no idea.

The rain—so darkly silver—
both cause and result. My drowned
body reciprocates. I have no secrets,
recall no lies.

If I could drag the ghosts from the wood,
if I could scrabble the ghosts,

if I could make the whisper
the learning curve of the rings...

So much for the songbirds
that made the tree fly away.

Seeing cuts the seen world in half
by weary strokes—the mirror told her
one thing, the dream another. So much
for math. The history of the stories
is the calculation under the divide.

Of course I will stop and see a tree,
from its roots or knees to the ways
it leans, patience personified

but trees are easy
beauty that stays put
that does not terrify or hear

So much like so many other days
the sky conceals its conclusions

The trick has always been
to assemble time and space so
they coincide
not a hundred years later
but now, the big now you
wake up in

There You Are

Sometimes I try to read the moon like a book
as if it were an old tree full of stories
stuck in the asphalt night
I laugh along with the moon at the names
we give it, the measures we take from its stoic
punctual self, the idea that an idea
born on earth could be of the slightest
moment to this big rock caught
in the net of our girth

For years, I tried to see the moon
through tree limbs—red bud, sycamore,
oak of course, pine, so many, all to catch
a glimpse of her complicity.
I was not convinced the moon wasn't
hearing it all—the songs chiefly,
wafting away from the mouth of pain (or
joy—mustn't deny it) toward trembling
ears, among them hers, the sly moon, the
uninvited one, clothed in cold light, her
pitted face half guarded by a silver scarf—

The moon has taken nothing away
Nothing from anyone
Let others make of the moon what they
will, legend or warning, arbiter of the wave
and the madness beneath
The moon's indifference is the key
The rest of us howl and dance

Here's a question: is the moon
sending secret messages to select dead
ones? There in the moist earth—fragments
of themselves—are they receiving
orders that read as music?

If the phases of that old woman, that cold
stone, that pocked mirror, that hanging

basket of shadows are connoting
anything, I do not believe it is the
unpardonable mystery you wish
to unbury...nor a chart
detailing the births of the fastest horses...
and not even a crooked glass corner down
the street from where you are going to die.
Let's call the phases she wheezes through
by the names of famous clowns, or
discontinued brands of smoke. That much
we can account for, trying to sleep.

On his way off the planet my friend said,
'Keep your eye on the moon, your poetry'

He was not an ancient poet of ancient
China, but a river seer, a physician of the
line between word and speech, between
sound and song, between sadness and
death. Steeled connoisseur of the ineffable—
dressed as a young man in a hurry. My
friend knew the moon as an equal. His
words made the moon pause and cast
a glance in my trembling direction. Oh.
There you are.
Said the clowning moon. Said the somber
stone. Said the brightness so softly
enfolding the time of my life on earth.

THE THRILL OF BEING THOUGHT OF IN TWO LANGUAGES

Possession of stolen things

You train yourself to think
Along lines plunging toward
Rivers of sorrow, seas of regret

But the oddest friction intervenes
Times against the whirl of it all

I think this time of Sunny
Years and years inside
Unable to see out at least in words
Perhaps not even longing for the change
Music— well or poorly played—can
Fix inside a tired brain
Something I can do
However sad, bereft, broken off prior
Understandings
                My old voice
No more special than this shirt
My daughter and her friend wrote on
Once in a welling of enthusiasm
Over something small, something to do to do with school

Rain Won't Solve Them Either

The song takes you down
to a place you cannot visit
where every day your skull cracks
like a melon in the hot dry sun,
the way she went away
requires thinking. Your own face
does not like you, after all,
and nothing but surrender suits
your failure to be any kind
of true—
           I worry that no past
is ever through taking down its
ornamentation, however meager,
vulgar, or divine.
We worm our way through apple
after apple, in it for the journey
and the food, careless of one
another and, so, rude.

IN A DIFFERENT LIFE

In a different life I might have
green vistas, a mountain, a sea,
attached time, someone
behind me putting a hand just right
(as happened once)

In the dream you made promises
that even in the dream you said,
shit, why did I promise that

Who knows what's back there
where your life was?

Once I followed my heart—
What a bad leader!
Bursts of angel fire,
Followed by betrayal
And misery

So happy
for such a short while
perfectly
normal progress
through
timed time

Grateful and afraid
Let the forgery
Find the vein

The trick is to act like you've got
All the time in the world

THAT PROPRIETARY RAG

I say Honey the Hobo got a raw deal
and that was before they stole his paper
bag full of rotting vegetables

and then the dead man reminded me
what was a poem and what was just
the leftover canopies at the damaged wedding

The damn fool thought he could live in
New Orleans, he imagined living there—
imagine!

Parked. With the window down and his feet up

Who can have these dreams? That is
to say, who is entitled to have them, not
who is able.

What to say about my great and sad friend
whom I barely knew?

Once—before the migration that brought me here—
maybe I could have wallowed
on the futility of Italian politics.

Mostly then I'm like an egg.
About to become something. Supposed to.
Cultured for an eventuality
already neglected, about to be lost,
not to begin with, either plain or
mysterious enough.

Most of America passes by in the dark.

The hollowed out heart would like
would like
would
like
to rejoice

PEACHES
for Mom

I haven't the moon's worth of sense it might take
to query my new state of mind, so
tack away brightly and sing your own song
while I fiddle a map out of darkest moonlight
to brick up a bad back
and make this dog's night go long

WHAT JOHN STOSS KNOWS

I understand these doors and windows
through which getting here
I got lost

You should see me when nobody can see me

the little light is

air all uprounded drumming

walking the high line with Stern
closer to heaven than usual (because
where I'm from, that patch on
perdition)—walking among the blessing
of many tongues, not to mention
talking in and of them (because
possible with an old chum)

I only traded sex for misery, and never
began anything with the ones I adored

nor did not stay lonely year upon year
but did I suffer?
or was it all the same to be among the living,
all welled deep and obscure

White people are funny
if you look at them the right way, if
you squint, and don't mind your bs
layered, if they don't mean to harm you
whether they mean to or not

No matter what I say
I know I'm going to miss earth
miss the sight of...everything but
especially
the garden of my children's minds

I learned from my brother John Stoss that
I don't need enemies, I also learned
that women are better human beings than
men, and that walking on soil is superior
to walking on pavement—what John
doesn't know does not need to be known.

WHEN IT BECOMES

No matter the smarts
they have to start over
the boy or girl the girl or boy
inventing fun, inventing heartache,
inventing the paths through the storm
and the storm itself, the boy-girl or the
girl-boy, opening the folds of the world
like a cardboard box that won't yield easy,
surprised as they have to be no matter
who has given the heads-up about what,
because down there they can't learn what
they don't know.
                    There's a reason
you can't tell them anything: you don't
know anything, or nothing they need
to know when they need to know it.

Waking Up Cold

Explosion of flowers, black petals flaming
Beatles flipped over
The underside of the female
Nothing turning red
Wavering light
People you have plans with
The clock being moved while
All stand still
Distant door
Eye numb, surprise bedding
Once there was you were there once
Possible ideas about the perimeter
Knife slip
Hold your horses
Of and about, listen

The Skin We're In

That fragment of speech we call a name...

We are all carrying mountains
of story in our pockets

The life of the poem is the life you're living
with its dark spots and decay
disguised, an incoherent hash
on the bounce, too full of heedless joy
and mute aftermath...

The light in the water or the water in the light—which?
Deprived of music, they become heartless.

Aware in the dream of my age and stoutness,
I let you embrace me. You did not
turn away, as in years past
or the dreams of years past. I had to wonder, waking,
was there meaning? But of course, no,
such is the dream, an underneath, an
end-stopped, a point on a rough stick
centered near your eye. Your eye. I said,
your eye.

Now I have mastered
I have only mastered
I am the master of
the art of being home

When you are listening to music, smoking cigarettes, high, with a glass in your
    hand full of promises, you don't want to live forever, be any more permanent
    than the smoke escaping your lips, prone to any lie that makes the single
    moment blast in through time, but as for lingering, no, you don't want it .

You can only meet up in your time, not before and not after. If someone curses at
    you because you didn't wait to be born, run, run
or wants you to wait a lifetime like a sentence that won't reach its necessary
    conclusion, fold.
Fade. Forget filling out
the form.

O doo da day

Absent artifacts, I can only swear
to what happened, as if
I knew. I'd never seen a person
erase her tracks while walking in them before. It was thrilling
like a long fall down from a height so high
you have time not to worry—
not to know how easily bones break, muscles fail, the whole she-bang
of your entwinement comes flying apart.

In the dream
nothing satisfied me—not anyone's
best efforts. I even questioned whether
those *were* their best efforts.
I wouldn't pick that up, I said of the
proposed object. I wouldn't even
pick that up.

And have I escaped the story or
the story me? Or absences, which
have I chosen, which have chosen me?

Will my world become
one unbroken cavalcade of images
melting around me?

The word 'whenever' separated generations—when I heard it,
I had to stop and think.

Tomorrow you'll have a different song in your head
I promise the curve of the curse of time
will leave you too breathless to sing it

Connected However to a Loving Other

In the beginning the screen was part of the door
where I lay content sipping juice
and looking out on the street—
even now, it holds in a porch

All manner of the tree spoke
The bird bearing honey and the bee song
The air itself a cauldron but still

The June bugs early
and the fireflies all gone out

It is best
for a monster to live
inside his head

Men At Seventy

They seem the same to me
(except the ones who've taken the plunge, of whom
I can't speak)—some fatter, some thinner,
some neither, slower maybe
(but than what?), less unruly hair, all
kinds of small superficial notes, 'tude
for instance where pacific natures ruled,
or shyness poking out where certainty
once occluded consciousness. We could talk
these measure out, I guess, and say
age changes those who wait for it (unlike
a few who said an early nevermind)...

WHO EXACTLY WE ARE

In this dream I'm in a small space capsule rocket but with a few others—we all wear colors (uniforms and body parts) that determine our role, status—our parts are removable/interchangeable—we are just taking off from a destination like Mars back to earth—there is a human young guy in charge of the ship's navigation and hardware and he's fooling with stuff, some of us are being critical of his choices— like there has been a completely other pathway which he might have made but he's telling us it's alright and at some point I'm aware of being in a small capsule hurtling through gorgeous empty space at lightning speed and I see it from out- side as well as inside—aware that even with full engine failure we'd fall for days, weeks before hitting anything solid—I am concerned for the stability that if my identity as my parts are interchangeable but then I see my name (Agdy or some- such) in a screen list of more common names and am reassured that somewhere is a master list of who exactly we are and I relax into the hurtling as the capsule seems to right itself and be in a steady intentional course.

My color is dark brown and I believe I may be a 'female.'

NO MARKINGS, NO COLLAR, NO CHIP

How bad a reader am I? Forty,
Fifty years in, I've yet to finish
Any of my favorite books.

'Part of the thing is bodies is bodies...'

Renter

naked we feel, unphoned—
lost in a world that can't find us

I think you could find me

I imagine climbing this rubbery event without you

One smelled of garlic—the other, celery.
My confusion was intrinsic and endemic...

It's almost always true
That you'll get over me
Before I get over you

Not All Bookies Die from a Gunshot to the Head

Our barber Augie must've also been
my father's bookie but
one day on the front page, he was dead.

A small man, balding, with a thin mustache is what I think I remember, and
small time too, I'm guessing
from his shop

(My Uncle Benny, small time bookie elsewhere in his youth did not die this way,
but lived long enough to die of liver cancer.)

After a haircut, interrupted a dozen times by the ringing phone, Augie would give
    us kids
a nickle, for our time

LIVING IN THE BLUE SCREEN

Who doesn't love a second chance, who
wouldn't ask for a third or a fourth,
do-overs *ad infinatum*...

People trying to be happy—

No purchase in the heart—

Worse is which:
the terror of being chosen
or the terror of not being
chosen?

The camera doesn't linger
and neither should we

DOING

My son is throwing his childhood away,
the parts he can still see, now crammed
into large garbage bags at the foot of the stairs,
not counting memories, of which he claims to have none
from our last two houses,
where he was zero to nearly twelve...

I used to dream myself into a big house,
so there were always new wings I hadn't been in before,
some cozy, some almost dormitory style—

A hundred years from now
when all the wars are 100 years
further in the past, as are we...

...every part of me sometimes agrees
the world makes no sense
and can't possibly be here
but then—

Childhood ends so slowly for the parent
and so abruptly for the child—

where is the here it can't be
though filled with blood
topped by bile
hanging from the thread of eyesight...

The things we never ask
that we always want to know
like where exactly was the house
my young father found a room

and what was the name of the old man
who woke him with a cup of coffee
every morning, pampering,
the way his big sister had done...

You remember
and then do,
remember again, and
then do, again, and remember
and so on, doing, until
you can't remember

AND YET MY HEART IS FULL

Who has the right
To reclaim the night?
Old man walking
On the end of a rope.

He tries
he fails
to squeeze the exquisite line
from the broken mouth

WHAT ALL STAYS INSIDE MY HEAD

What you have to live with grows
exactly as you do—

When it comes to food
a lot of the time
I think what we're eating is memories—

I lean toward envy, inhaling the dark lake
of all my failures
until aspiration chokes me—

Knowing what to light
and what to cut away, yeah?

You're the dog in my coffee
You're the spoon in my sleep

I don't know how (not) to sit still

A man who sleeps in the clothes he has worn all day
(minus pants and shoes)
the rich history of the parents, almost completely forgotten

Everything comes to an end, which is why
beginnings are over-rated, as is
setting foot outside your nest

when

anymore is fifteen divided by three
shaped like a 'y'

II. UNCLAIMED BODIES

*"You know you've gotten old
when you leave your house in the morning
not expecting to fall in love."*

—*attributed to
Howard Nemerov*

About Blank

Lost love at twenty, let's see, where were we...?
Already the balloon had taken the fatal hit, already
Too late... so back a further trifle we go, back
One more year to a darkly different story but one
In which flesh follows flesh in the way of all
Who have everything and the fragrance of it, and
Great long clusters of arpeggios rising and
Falling, nothing but the raw pure honey descending
Or the singular songbird, lonely lookout, arising.

You know a thing is doomed by how you covet it
Despite it is right there in your reach, in fact,
Within your touch, the sweetest imaginable taste,
The gaze uninterrupted by introspection, beyond
The idiot catcall of doubt, right where if one were
Not a stupid human creature with no memory and no
Fear, one might hear the foreign whisper, the softly
Hammered click of the chambering. Pow!

EVERYTHING DIES THAT'S A FACT

The end of things to go wrong is not in sight
This is no fly on a broomstick watching us
The dog does not trot freely in the street
All hell is the hospital, or the morgue and
It is not going anywhere, licked by frenzy
For the end of time, the hint of violin in
Your voice. (I did say it again, the second
Person absent or imaginary or just mad.)

Half a life ago—bewildered by sadness so
Present and so unknown, helped to sleep
By drink and the absence of any future—
The train goes without me trailing words
I can't hear despite how familiar they sound
Kindness has gotten up and left the arena
Where my heart laid promiscuously bare
Its vast ignorance, its river-drowned point
Of view, its locality. Sadness pre-dating
And on a winning streak, the worst kind,
Yearning abandoned, everything broken
Half-past the dog's whisker, no home
Coming, all the good hiding places fatal—
Many a moonlight moment lingers, air
Finally cooling, the breadth of the drink
Not yet sunk in, almost could feel warm
Dog curled around that cold foot, oh
Remember the song, dammit, the one
Approaching August in outer space, laughing
Was possible, almost guaranteed, and death.

WHERE

I hear the drums knocking
Over the mandolin
The lips so versatile
I want to be all the ears

Everywhere hearing less
In a world I won't see
To drown the voice
In my ear. Is the solitary

Last knock of the drum
The bell that will ask
Where are you going
When here was always

Dream Comfort Memory Despair

I can see the tops of trees from a thousand feet
Covered by blue salt
Through which raining I fall

There is something hot breaking our bones
The flowers don't help
Waving like tiny red corals
At the bottom of the sea

Love is coming, disguised,
Brittle as oyster shell in the sun
Torn like a flyer or the poor man's shirt
On a guitar riff strung out
Past the known galaxies

Face it is the worst advice
Would a monarch take it?
Affirmative growl from underground
Notwithstanding which stands
On its own. The vibration hurts
My fall. My hand stretches to the wind.

THIS ISN'T THE END

Like a stain dropping into your sleep
air will find you unbreathed longing last
rubbery concoction loneliness which
letter to favor in eternity snaps better

I'll take my time all the time thinking
the wailing whistle waffles while we
ruin devastation itself a tiny spot
in the sun's eye, nothing that we knew

looking up to the friendly moon humming
some absence ago. Dirt became us
burning liquors love pours into and over
each and every free loose wasting fool

cut strings gut speed hollow willow
adore you piping hot bedframed
length of the tree in deep union under
ground the faces all eye and finding you.

The Suggestion Keeps Changing

For instance, you take a dog.
The story you withhold is the one.
Next, expectations of the rain.

The river has no heart, just a soul.
The fallen hand finds a way in.
After the story, rich silence.

Equinox, if you must.
Keep the speech inside margins.
Visually, hold it out.

Sing within the barrows of the song.
Covering what you can with eyes closed.
Don't be lonely, don't cry.

The end will cover your hands like fur.
You might ask, whose voice is calling me.
The cat runs funny, sails catching wild wind.

IF NOTHING WAS WORRYING YOU, WOULD YOU

Climb into that cave
Release the sounds

A young guy with nothing but what-all on his shoulders must go to war
He must carry a rifle which he must also shoot upon command

All of which never gets fixed
Time being a bitch in heat

Worse than the usual threat of death is the goddamned mud
Inside the broken boot and the way food stinks in your mouth

All the words were given me by you
The screaming is my own and so quiet

Before he can save himself he must save at least a dozen
Younger, no downtown in this sob story, all hell kneels

But from a window medium high
The disappearance is visible

Traded for living through it all any sense of place
Or time for the simple love of an ordinary day

O the song may even sing itself
This dream long this departure

What the foxhole hides is freezing men, now animal
Owing to mad edicts and the crime of government

If one could cold hold love
Like a book, a simple weight

Feet to face they sleep awaiting dawn
The past in every dream going south

Awaiting a Word

In Refuge a young woman spoke
To me (!) apropos my name dangling
(Foolishly I'd say) and I put on
My old man manners—polite, reserved,
Too surprised to speak as me—
She was there for a funeral, some
Relation I didn't catch and staying
With a sister who mapped for Google
The very city to which neither of us
Belonged—we were just getting coffee
After all, or I was; she was getting hot
Chocolate for three and a doughnut—
And yes, the fact is, after we said
That thing about having a nice day,
And went out into the sunlight,
I spent the next one looking for her,
Hopelessly but the kind of hopeless
That is merely the absence of expectation.
Who says hello anyway to a stranger?
The pony tail was pure afterthought.

The Blues (Comes Close)

Water is blue in our dreams
And language.

     Cast off.

A baby might reasonably ask at the outset
how can I learn enough in the little time left.

Lay away the song, so flight can rearrange
What you are and are not now

Doing the math one calculates stiffness.
Circular motion. Much crackling.

     Skin like mold.

You hear the welcome deep in the throat.
The shyness, loosed of all weight of the past.

Instead, the song finds the road, while
What do you think times does, you think it passes?

Home crushed by music we light out
The vernacular of free space unfamiliar

So much traveling without any leaving,
Exiled into one's own heart, rats!

     Some space.

Is it time we ask is it time again and
Is it already time present past future

     Grudging etceteras.

I could count backwards from childhood
If I wanted a better glimpse of sun and moon

The dice get thrown in carefully cleaned corners
But come up snake eyes every (time!), ah

It doesn't take long for the bug to climb your arm,
What's that on the table beside your shadow? uh oh

      I mean.

Really all I wanted was to have the words
Dripping off me, plenty time I woke up

Scared, and out of them, out of everything
Climbing the air where you are not

Turns out I lost while the pots kept coming
My way. Did we not share the rain at least

Once? My house is full of old men,
None of them smiling, neither hand nor foot

Lost in the net nest of love, the nest net
How to surrender, world of mine

      Times see.

Who could not have rendered farewell better?
Under the weight of the whole earth, some regret

      Blue stop.

Taking Me There

One thing is certain I am not white. Thank God for that.
It makes everything else bearable.

—Bob Kaufman

'ZEN TREE JOY, DAD'

In one day, counting night, I see my brother what's left of him now sporting (there is an odd word here) a white mustache but only close to the lip, realizing I don't know how to do this it's not like playing the piano which I also cannot do and then to have the dream in which we are at ease more remarkably because some of my family some friends are also there but you are cool and just want to talk with me alone and we are about to when it is morning, raining, time

'CREATION IS PERFECT'

Was it loved this book with brown circling each page just ahead of brittle now opening another dead poet for my ignorance to feast on that old man must have sat in his room in a perpetual scribble mode saying two words over and over to himself no longer there and someone before me who loved the book if the author didn't wrote helpfully in a margin 'too self-pitying?' movement interrupted by the political when a lone horn strikes

'GENETIC COMPLICATIONS'

Oh that's a ride great is the useless poet he has conquered seven dream cycles still bright minds entertain god and will be about setting the rows straight squeezing tight a small finding while the young pagans of two and three mill about in their ecstatic absence of privacy and the dog eats unspeakable stuff from the floor we are not here anymore my loves nor is it clear in the far enchantment we were

'COLD COLD PAGES, WAITING'

a strange noise, clacking? modifies the beat and don't that beat all hell's a mouth wanting a kiss far from any highway from any field or woods away in the lost light hunter without a prayer suddenly I needed the sound of a voice whether putting forth ideas or songs or even just a dumb remark itself miracle where the market is open for blood, where the farewell is what travels

MY POEM IN WHICH HOPE EXISTS

Just to be alive on earth and walk down to the water
Just to have the sound of it in your ears, and to wish
Food in the bellies of all the earth's people, now, and whenever
They are hungry. Such a simple place, earth, if we subtract
The worst things in each of our hearts, if we become
Generous in the same way trees are, giving away everything
While standing firm not indifferent to color or light but
Taking them in the friendly hug of time and space until
The thing earth wants from us, our sharp minds in service
Our hands working but able to rest and the breath of billions
Exhaling easily in the evening breeze in the heart of the home we share
Should share in equal measure and with no further rancor
Drawn by water, made one with the waters wandering ways
Whole like new like each and all births renew us and we keep

Fairhope, March 2019

How to Communicate with the Light

First, keep moving light under
Stands speed
As lonely as the light is, take
The moon
Search for air the search
For air will go longer
Has not been called
On account of light
Looks back at you from your feet
Up. How the light hits you
That clinches it
How much water must
Cover over
Inside the earth, rebellion, a missed
Tick, oh!
Who can look at this note passing over us
And not break into song?

He Who Has Stalled

I

Young is a different set of facts
A different kind of smile
It's crazy-making to hear
Truth emerge from inexperience

There we were
Hanging all the bad
True ideas mixing it up
Lifelong fears corporalising

A thing, as it happens, of little concern
The ver wors thing that could happen
Like it or not like it r not
Unhand me someone cries out
Into the universe
Why I never

This will do for destination
Nearing the end of the alphabet

Instead of wanting to eat I want
My ears flooded with sound
If some of that noise is music, man,
I'm satisfied

II

The heartbeat of a perimeter
Such a waste of ignorance
Refined, aloes of gold,
driving the feeble brain to frenzy
batting against the intransigent skull
so much whittling, or for whittling

How the muscles pluck their own
Strings languidly. How sleep
Is thinner than the moon.

We've always need water.
I could say what, wait or wait, what

A beast has the only idea
Stick around and see what's next
Control nothing what do you think you are more
Important than a leaf, than your cousin the cricket

When we say come on to one another, oh
Come on, what sort of invitation is it?
Let us go, the boss said, and make our visit

THE OLD LIFE

Maybe the one thing should be the other
sidewalks were softer songs coming back from nowhere
who wants to hear an argument about bourbon in a normal tone of voice
there's only one answer to your skin
3 thieves and a ton of money and drop your hands
It's alright it was a flurry of eerie baby baby

The aliens used to be a lot more interested in us
thousands more incidents of rock 'n roll
who can remember the day of the schism? schisms?
A rich man was deciding what he wanted to do with his life
having already taken
                                        all the time in the world
he thought he might wipe out ugliness

the bullet travels in the classic son of a classic arc
toward honey with its lifetime guarantee
of what comes next comes back comes on blushed
opposite from the eye's apple or the heart's
old fashioned fissure alongside the lake
pausing where the blueprint bleeds off the page

In 1944 all the leaders of the War looked weary
on the verge of sudden death to tell the truth
not knowing what to say when the knives came out
which disaster to consume and call it 'our song'
there is no one to take your place it seems
every man bows to the lost woman of the lost song

The day of the sensible report has passed
Our hearts hang in a future tense seeded
melancholy you say she can't tell a this from a that
as the levels descend the hero becomes more informed
and so we believe the great artist simply couldn't see
what have the bells and the horror brought us to

With no privacy and no ambition the baby is free
to remember
                    everybody held their breath
clearly it is cowboy songs that have made the population crazy
you think of the men holding back history with their bloody hands
with whatever bodies trying to keep the wind from blowing or the sea
from making waves oh the hours of our lives that are wasted
time not for you or for me
                    for rolling forward or standing still

This Is How I Leave

We've met like this dozens of times I say
35 you correct blowing softly on your nails
not looking up...

I think of all the women I've known
at their sexiest
not necessarily their youngest

(Carolyn's hips walking into a crowd for instance, under the summer weight cloth)
I was in this house once
a man was dying in the front room near the water
while his sons came and went

Then we had everything
with nothing jammed up inside of it

I don't know if I'm dreaming you
more present or more absent
but you are there most nights now,
away as I return.

I'm not smart enough to write poetry
I don't know what the words mean
especially as you receive them

Put up enough bridges and pretty soon
you have an old building pocked with windows

Will you want me to have done it differently?
is the one fear I can't shake off—

It's hard to look at a thing straight on
though even then what you see is
distortion so you might as well
keep the glance economical, unclear

I might have regretted it before.
I don't think I regret it anymore.

I'd say so if I were me, put
the broken pieces back together.

Poetry is how you keep one foot out of the grave.

(I said that)

Wooden Steps, Big People

The need to eliminate—instead a cavern deep
and artful opens just there where I am falling
not asleep sleep is easy but waking up
and just any old way is not for the faint-hearted
no more than keeping your eyes closed is ever
a good strategy when something touches
the skin or tricks the ear open
do all old men talk about not being old
because they've forgotten? The way we used to
say we had eaten something that didn't
agree with us. The dog will want more anytime
anyplace who were you talking to
he'll want the blanket for over the
sheet for under I see the treacherous steps
they are actually stone don't want to follow
you forever but still even so wait wait wait
but wait then there's a chicken dancing
on that grainy floor the trees have so much to do
but the dog can't leave my side
as sense must go now every last blockade
exploded from the inside galling the antagonism
of having forgotten unfamiliar smells what
happened to the gods when people stopped
talking about them you know this
raised to be such a one as keeps only elegant company
let's put our hands together now for water

I Say Hi-Dee to Frank, Bread Dry As Paper

Those thinking about doing the things I have done, go ahead,
and add a few too

The world I think I'm living in
is taking the 'A' train

When you're younger you think the past
goes away, but it never does

The closer you get to it, the less
it looks like the pictures,
radically less

But you have to be a regular somewhere
kidding the form
nowhere to go, no way to get there

All those loose ends, all the time.
Drowning in them.

Time consuming.
Cuddle, muddle, huddle.

I come by my track face honestly,
nobody's best shot at happiness.

❖❖❖

The rhythm of my work
suits me said the smith,
the space inside the days
the nights that come between—
most times I hit the mark
and when I don't I don't
dwell on the mistake.

❖❖❖

You don't dare look at your hands
anymore...if your name is Guillaume
Apollinaire, but you do because you're
you, you see...

❖❖❖

At heart : a kind of
helpless indifference.

Seventy: not ready
to play an old man.

I love what's mine,
claiming nothing.

No aging
out of the blues.

❖❖❖

Hey Frank can I get my father's suitcase back it's kind of a relic (or will be two
    years from now)...

You want to tap on the glass and open the door (in four years of living in five
    apartments in that town I never had a key) and walk in on that tense tri-alogue
maybe spill something for the distraction maybe redirect the conversation
    toward jazz
music beyond words as words are not doing anyone any good here and now,
    maybe
tap one of them on the shoulder to say hey we'll all feel better tomorrow and—
    um, ulp, etc—
tomorrow is another day. But of course, who'd have heard me in that brilliant
    room
crawling with dense intellect & mad creativity? The silences alone must have been
like the 6:30 to Memphis exploding down the track (not that anything but craftily
    disguised
poisonous freight cars ever passed through here, rattling the glasses on the tables
at George's Majestic Lounge). Or yeah, I could've said let's get the hell outta here,
    head
down to George's for some beer and I could use a meatball sub, having traveled
    through time

like this, what the hell, you guys, it's just—what is it 'just'?—it's just

betrayal, pride, the detritus of lies, some failure of a simple heart rounding
a base, nothing

to die over or give up the slender thread of love that binds us, angry as we are, or
sad,

or determined to give up and go away... or even just *done*, because there is another
surprise

coming—you're a smart guy, Frank, you know all this, WTF (an abbreviation we'll
all be using

in the world you'll never see), put the gun down, have another, look at that god-
damn moon!

Hi-dee, Frank! what a night, man, I thought... shit, not even going to say what I
thought.

ACKNOWLEDGEMENTS

The author extends his grateful acknowledgement to the editors and publishers of the following journals and anthologies where some of these poems first appeared:

The Maple Leaf Rag VI (Portals Press) — "Pre-Sleep" and "This Is Now"

40th Anniversary Anthology of the Maple Leaf Poetry Readings (Portals Press) — "Prewriting Isaac's Elegy"

Redactions #22 (Redactions Poetry & Poetics) — "Unclaimed Bodies" and "The Last Thing We Ever Do"

Valley Voices (Mississippi Valley State University) — "Morning That Held Sway," "Rain Won't Solve Them Either," and "Diary of Wind and Weather"

The Night's Magician: Poems About the Moon (Negative Capability Press) — "There You Are"

Constant Stranger: After Frank Stanford (Foundlings Press) — "There You Are"

In addition, I want to thank Joe Phillips and Susan Wood of Black Widow Press for taking this book on, and especially one of its editors, Geoff Munsterman, for his tact and finesse, patience and encouragement.

I also thank my employer, Xavier University, for the sabbatical during which the second part of this book was written. And Allison and the crew at Gracious for the shelter of a clean, well-lighted place.

And as always, my family—Kay, Jack and Ezra—for giving me space in which to scribble—loved and secure. Thanks. I would be speechless without you.

Ralph Adamo was born, raised and educated in New Orleans, and except for the four years he spent in Fayetteville, Arkansas's U of A MFA program, has lived there his entire life. He is the author of seven previous collections, beginning in 1972 with *The Tiger Who Spoke French*. His work also appears in many journals and anthologies, among them *Contemporary poetry in America* (Random House), *The Made Thing: An Anthology of Contemporary Southern Poetry* (U. of Arkansas Press), *American Diaspora: The Poetry of Exile* (U. of Iowa Press), *Another South: Experimental Writing in the South* (U. of Alabama Press), as well as LSU Press's *Uncommonplace: An Anthology of Contemporary Louisiana Poets*.

The recipient of a NEA fellowship, a Louisiana Division of the Arts Individual Artist Grant, and winner of the first-ever Pirate's Alley William Faulkner Society Marble Faun Award for poetry, Ralph has taught creative writing at Xavier, Tulane, LSU, and Loyola.

In the mid-70s, Ralph co-edited, with Louis Gallo and Ellen Gilchrist, *Barataria*, a short-lived but prominent independent literary magazine in New Orleans. He also edited the literary journal *New Orleans Review* (NOR) in the 90s and is the current editor of *Xavier Review* and Xavier Review Press.

He and his wife Kay two have children, Jack and Ezra.

BLACK WIDOW PRESS POETRY IN TRANSLATION

In Praise of Sleep: Selected Poems of Lucian Blaga by Lucian Blaga
Translated by Andrei Codrescu

Through Naked Branches: Selected Poems of Tarjei Vesaas by Tarjei Vesaas
Translated by Roger Greenwald

I Have Invented Nothing: Selected Poems by Jean-Pierre Rosnay
Translated by J. Kates

Fables of Town & Country by Pierre Coran
Translated by Norman R. Shapiro & Illustrated by Olga Pastuchiv

Earthlight (Clair de terre): Poems by André Breton
Translated by Bill Zavatsky and Zack Rogow

The Gentle Genius of Cecile Perin: Selected Poems (1906-1956) by Cecile Perin
Translated by Norman R. Shapiro

Boris Vian Invents Boris Vian: A Boris Vian reader
Edited and Translated by Julia Older with a Preface by Patrick Vian

Forbidden Pleasures: New Selected Poems [1924-1949] by Luis Cernuda
Translated by Stephen Kessler

Fables In a Modern Key (Fables Dans L'Air Du Temps) by Pierre Coran
Translated by Norman R. Shapiro & Illustrated by Olga Pastuchiv

Exile Is My Trade: A Habib Tengour Reader by Habib Tengour
Translated by Pierre Joris

Present Tense of The World: Poems 2000-2009 by Amina Said
Translated by Marilyn Hacker

Endure: Poems by Bei Dao
Translated by Clayton Eshleman and Lucas Klein

Curdled Skulls: Poems of Bernard Bador by Bernard Bador
Co-translated and edited by Clayton Eshleman

Pierre Reverdy: Poems Early to Late by Pierre Reverdy
Translated by Mary Ann Caws and Patricia Terry

Selected Prose and Poetry of Jules Supervielle by Jules Supervielle.
Translated by Nancy Kline, Patrica Terry, and Kathleen Micklow

Poems of Consummation by Vicente Aleixandre
Translated by Stephen Kessler

A Life of Poems, Poems of a Life by Anna de Noailles
Translated by Norman R. Shapiro

Furor & Mystery and Other Poems by Rene Char
Translated by Mary Ann Caws and Nancy Kline

The Big Game (Le grand jeu) by Benjamin Péret
Translated by Marilyn Kallet

BLACK WIDOW PRESS MODERN POETS AND BIOGRAPHY

9 781733 892421